TABLE ⊂

ACKNOWLEDGMENTS

With our sincerest gratitude, we'd like to thank all those who contributed to the completion of this book. Thank you, Becky, Cathy, Debby, Dennis, Francine, Jean, Kelley, Lee, Lisa, Maria, Michele, Sharon, and Vanessa. A very special thank you to Jean Pierce, whose late-night editing was priceless!

CHAPTER 1
Introduction

"Too often we underestimate the power of a touch, a smile, a kind word, a listening ear, an honest compliment, or the smallest act of caring, all of which have the potential to turn a life around."

~ Leo Buscaglia ~
American author and motivational speaker
1924-1998

For well over forty years, through triumph and tragedy, success and failure, comfort and poverty, our relationship has endured and flourished while others have failed.

Over these years, we have learned and lived by what we now call our 15 Rules. By practicing these basic principles, we have thrived in our relationship, which grows stronger every day. In sharing our experience and strategy, we hope these 15 Rules will help to provide a foundation to assist you in developing your own loving, lasting, and satisfying relationship.

A word of caution: It's not going to work if one person is 100% committed and following the Rules, while the other partner is not. We see these Rules as an all-or-nothing proposition. You can't pick and choose. Following most of the Rules won't work. If you are truly looking for a loving, lasting, and satisfying relationship, you and your partner must be totally committed to every Rule.

In the following chapters, we hope to give you some insight into finding the right partner, and equally as important, establishing Rules that will create a foundation for a lasting relationship that will enhance each other's lives.

So, how about the listed order of these Rules? Are there some that are more important than others? The answer is no. Although some Rules may be more difficult to master, each is a "must" and is essential to a loving, lasting, and satisfying relationship.

At this point, you may be asking who we are, and what our credentials are. To start, we both have college degrees and successful careers in healthcare administration. Our expertise in relationships, however, goes back to our forty-plus years together and our nearly sixty years on this planet.

Each of us came from humble beginnings; as children, we were innocent victims of poverty, hunger, alcoholism, domestic abuse, and divorce. Like many unfortunate children, we dealt with the consequences of adults who *definitely* did not follow these Rules. Perhaps these experiences were the key to our success: we each became educated about the many mistakes that constitute a poor relationship. More importantly, our respective pasts possibly led us to a better understanding of what a loving, lasting, and satisfying relationship really means.

It probably comes as no surprise to you that, in present times, successful relationships are rare. When we look globally, the statistics are nearly identical, with 40-50% of marriages ending in divorce in most of Western civilization. The majority of those marriages end in less than eight years (Jegede, 2019) - yet our relationship remains strong.

Okay, so now you might be thinking that even though our childhoods were tough, we probably 'skated' through our relationship and had it easy. However, that is far from the

3

truth. In fact, we faced many circumstances and situations that severely tested our relationship's fortitude:

- In the early years of our marriage, we often floated bad checks for food just to make it to payday.
- We built a business and lost it in an ugly patent battle with a major healthcare company, resulting in us being left in tremendous debt.
- In Iraq, our son's tank hit an improvised explosive device (IED), leaving him with severe injuries.
- Our adult daughter lost her life in a tragic motorcycle accident.

These are just a few of the many relationship stressors we have endured.

Even just one of these circumstances has led many other relationships to crumble, yet our relationship remains strong.

Many of our friends, family, and colleagues have asked us the same question: How do we find a relationship like yours?

As you read this book, we hope you get a better understanding of who we are, and more importantly, what we have discovered to be the keys to a loving, lasting, and satisfying relationship. We hope you enjoy it.

CHAPTER 2

Rule #1
Be Best Friends

"The best and most beautiful things in the world cannot be seen or even touched - they must be felt with the heart."

~ Helen Keller ~
American Author
1880-1968

*L*ike, love, and *lust* are three powerful, distinct, and often confusing emotions when it comes to choosing a life partner. Each one may wax and wane over the years of a relationship; however, they are all equally important. So, as a guy might say (or probably ought to say to himself more often), let's analyze each of these *very different* emotions using our big-heads!

During many mornings in the factory's research and development department, Steve and his fellow workers toiled away while discussing a myriad of topics from the mundane, to deep philosophical questions, and everything in between. This morning was no different.

"Your wife is your best friend? That's so sad," Steve's supervisor, Bob, said to him during a 'meaning of life' group discussion.

"What?" Steve replied in amazement to Bob, who Steve knew as a very pleasant and openly religious man. "Your wife isn't *your* best friend?"

"No, of course not," Bob quickly responded. "That's not right." The other men quickly chimed in, each of them cackling in a chorus of agreement with Bob.

"No, it's sad that your wife *isn't* your best friend," Steve responded in utter astonishment, as he read the faces of his coworkers, who each looked deeply saddened and worried for what they perceived was Steve's lonely life.

Despite what this 'amateur therapy group' thought, friendship is the absolute key to happiness in a relationship. After all, doesn't everyone want to feel loved and appreciated? We all need someone with whom we can share stories, have a good laugh, and share common interests. We need a friend to lend support when we are down or when we are going through a tough time. We need a friend who knows our flaws, weaknesses, and quirks firsthand, yet loves us anyway. Best friends share these types of relationships. A loving, lasting, and satisfying relationship is one where each partner *is* a best friend to the other—this is a must.

Growing up, you may have had that one special best friend, or perhaps you had more than one. Sometimes these relationships last a lifetime, and sometimes they come and go. Your best friend may have been a neighbor, a cousin, or a school acquaintance. You may have one now; if you do, you are blessed.

Having one or more close friends is one of the best gifts in life. Prestige or financial riches aren't what warm the heart; what does do it is the richness of a laugh with a close friend during memorable times, or a hug from the same when you are in the midst of a temporary struggle. True friendship is where *like* and *love* go hand-in-hand—it's human kindness at its very best.

Working towards this type of relationship with your wife, husband, or partner is the key to your happiness, their happiness, and to a loving and lasting relationship. If you are in a relationship now and contemplating whether to 'pop the question,' or are wondering if this is someone you'd like to spend the rest of your days with, ask yourself, "Is this someone who lives up to the *best friend* standard?"

However, a life commitment goes even beyond a best friend standard. If you decide this is the right person for you, you will be spending far more time with this person than you would probably ever spend with a best friend.

Ask yourself, "Do I truly *like* this person—not *love*, but *like?*" Then ask yourself, "Considering my partner's words and actions, does he or she truly *like* me?" Then, repeat this for *love*. One without the other doesn't work. Your relationship must have both.

Then consider that with the commitment of a marriage, you are legally and morally agreeing in writing to spend THE REST OF YOUR LIFE with this person for BETTER OR WORSE. Choose wisely with your heart, and as we mentioned earlier, with your big head.

Friendship and love are not only about what your partner does to enhance your life, but what you give to enhance his or her life. More specifically, in a *best friend* relationship, your pleasure should also come in giving your partner pleasure. When you do, be grateful for the small things in return: a smile, a thank you, a warm hug, even a loving nod. Sometimes these little things are all it takes to get you to want to give and give again.

Now, before your mind wanders off as we throw the word *pleasure* around, you need to understand that good relationships are much more than lust, parties, and good sex. Don't deny it; you were thinking of sex as soon as you saw the word pleasure. Hold on. We will get to the *lust* piece a little later. Remember, big head thinking here.

Simpler pleasure comes from some of the less complicated times in a relationship. For example, pleasure is that warm feeling you get when the person you *like* and *love* is:

- Sitting with you on a long drive in the car or on a motorcycle.
- Lying next to you in bed or on a blanket, soaking up the sunshine.
- Giving or receiving a hug or a gentle touch.
- Engaging in good conversation about your weekend plans or your big life plans.
- Happy that you made dinner and excited about your new recipe or maybe sharing a warm laugh about how awful your new concoction came out.
- Watching a Hallmark movie or a football game with you and actually *paying attention*.
- Listening and helping you deal with a difficult day at work or home.

Undoubtedly, there could be plenty more examples like these. These kinds of moments are where friendship becomes a combination of *love* and *like*.

After stating that there is no order in which these Rules should go, it's important to emphasize that *love* and *lust* can only go so far. A relationship with just these elements will have an expiration date. Relationships don't last without you genuinely *liking* your partner and without you and your partner working at being liked. The 14 remaining Rules in this book are your keys to best friendship, being loved, and loving.

It Takes Two to Tango

If you are already in a relationship that isn't what you think it should be, if you are unhappy, or if you are searching for a new or better relationship, this *best friend* rule and the remaining 14 rules are a guide to improving *yourself* and making *you* someone who can be liked, loved, and even lusted after. Improving yourself is *your* contribution to improving your current relationship or finding a new, healthier relationship.

On the other hand, if you are reading this together with your partner that's even better, because you both will have a better understanding of these Rules for friendship and a lasting relationship.

Friend with Benefits

Let's try to get this out of the way early... *Sex!* We all know sex is most often an important part of a relationship and often a deal-breaker when there is disagreement; therefore, we can't avoid having a conversation about sex and how it pertains to your relationship. Let's get it on!

They say sex sells, and it does. Much too often, couples get caught in the drama and romance they see every day on television and in the media. Perhaps you met your significant other because one of you was attracted to the other over *lust*. It's okay; animal attraction and hungry eyes are human nature.

But a lasting relationship is being *friends* first—with benefits. Too often, lust is confused with love. Those are two *totally* different things. Focus, here!

How do you get to be liked, loved, and lusted after, and how do you learn to like, love, and lust after your current partner? Or, how do you find someone who you can like, love, and lust after?

The first answer is that you must be likable, lovable, and lust-worthy, yourself. Understand that drama and intrigue aren't part of a healthy relationship; yet, too often drama manages to creep into a relationship from one or both participants.

We've all met physically attractive people who are in reality, ugly. Beauty and good looks resonate from the inside, from the heart. Yes, to the best of your ability you should take care of your health and physical appearance, but also be loving, likable, warm, friendly, helpful, charming, positive, complimentary, and encouraging — true beauty is demonstrated by those who show human love and respect ... and a person with all these traits is damn sexy!

To illustrate, we need look no further than to the 1960's television show, *Gilligan's Island*. Despite being considered a sex symbol, Tina Louise and her character, Ginger, consistently lost out in popularity to her counterpart Dawn Wells who played 'plain Jane,' girl-next-door, Mary Ann. Wells received the most fan mail, and her character was consistently considered the most desirable in polls, year after year (Wikipedia.com, Gilligan's Island).

Be loving, a true friend, and yes, if you are in a consenting adult relationship, and if your partner (i.e., best friend) is asking for a 'benefit' once in a while, be willing according to your comfort level and time constraints. Compromise and negotiate if you must. Being a friend to your partner is being helpful when he or she has any kind of need. In the end, this consideration makes for a better relationship.

Consequently, if you are fortunate enough to be given the green light for a benefit, you should make this a mutually enjoyable experience because that's what friends do. If it's you who is asking, and it's you who has the itch that needs scratching, your goal should be to make your 'best friend' *very* grateful that he or she chose to 'roll in the hay' with you.

How do I learn to be a better friend for those opportunities when given the green light? Communicate. Learn what your partner likes, practice (with them, not someone else!), communicate, learn, repeat!

Friendship is the Key

The 19th Century German philosopher and scholar, Friedrich Nietzsche, couldn't have said it any better: *"It is not lack of love, but a lack of friendship that makes unhappy marriages."* Whether you are already married, contemplating marriage, or in another type of relationship, it is most important to make time for each other. Take time to talk, laugh, share, experience, and yes, to love your best friend—your partner. Start today; start now. Make it a point every day, every hour, be your partner's best friend. Get ready! Oh, it's gonna be fun.

CHAPTER 3
Rule #2
Be All-In

"Only one who devotes himself to a cause with his whole strength and soul can be a true master. For this reason, mastery demands all of a person."

~ Albert Einstein ~
German-born physicist, developer Theory of Relativity
1879-1955

I f you are already married, there is better than a 50/50 chance you will divorce (Jegede, 2019). In any relationship, statistically, the odds aren't good. All isn't lost, however, so don't throw in that towel just yet. A healthy relationship like ours *is* obtainable with sincere commitment. It's not a 50/50 commitment; it's a 100% commitment from *both* parties. You and your partner gotta be all-in.

Before we begin our discussion of being all-in, however, let us give you one quick caveat: Being all-in with your partner doesn't mean that you should deprive others, such as your children and extended family members, of your attention. Your relationship can have your *full* attention, without having *all* of it.

Money for Nothing …

Have you ever had "that" co-worker who is a master at slacking off? Perhaps you are working with one right now? You know, we're talking about that person who works incredibly hard at doing just the minimum—hardly nothin'—to stay employed. There is at least one in every factory, office, store, etc. who, to your amazement, stays employed. He or she is the one for whom you and your co-workers are "bustin' your tails" to overcome his or her shortcomings. You know, someone who wouldn't consider reading a self-help book like this one, because they think they already have all the answers. Drives you crazy, right?

If you are at work now, go ahead and look over at that slacker; glare at him or her! Just kidding; that isn't nice. Of course, if you are at work reading this, we hope *you* are on a coffee break; otherwise, *you* might be that slacker! Just kidding again. Nonetheless, this is a perfect example of someone who isn't 100% committed to a promise he or she made to his or her employer.

Relationships are the same. Some folks are 100% committed, and some are slackers. You probably know some relationship slackers yourself.

We hate to say it, but perhaps you are glaring at your partner right now. Yeah, your partner, who may be innocently sitting near you watching a television program, wondering what the hell they've done wrong now, because we've just convinced you that your partner may be a relationship slacker. Wait! Before you rush to judgment, let's look at this subject a little more intently.

Lead by Example

Improving or fortifying a lasting relationship starts with you. You must be dedicated to an all-in, 100% commitment. Take personal responsibility for your relationship; dedicate yourself to adhering to the 15 Rules presented in this book, and lead by example. There is no guarantee that your partner will follow your lead; however, setting an example is doing *your* part, and doing your part is the best you can do.

You often hear that you can't change another person's behavior, that 'tigers do not change their stripes.' Later in this book, we emphasize that you should not start a relationship thinking you can change your partner's behavior. Nevertheless, whether you are a parent, a leader in your field, a manager, a co-worker, or a coach, you'll find that leading by example often has a significant influence on human behavior.

As leaders in the field of healthcare, both of us have witnessed and experienced dramatic, positive changes in organizations. A significant reason for that positive change started with those in leadership positions leading by example. This leadership was especially crucial when it came to improvement in employee morale and customer service. Therefore, if this method works so well with a company's employees, then why wouldn't you want to try it on your partner?

We can't guarantee that committing yourself to lead by example and following our 15 Rules will change that partner you might still be glaring at, but we *can* guarantee that without your all-in, 100% commitment, your relationship is likely doomed to fail regardless of your partner's involvement.

So, what is 100% commitment? Well, first, it is a commitment to the 15 Rules laid out in this book. When God laid out the Ten Commandments to Moses at Mount Sinai, we doubt God said to him, "Do your best to follow these rules" *or* "I'd be satisfied if you score a 7 or 8." If our Sunday School memory serves us well, these were all-in, 100% committed rules. No exceptions.

Yes, we know, we've stepped it up a bit with 15 Rules. Nevertheless, our experience has demonstrated that nothing less than 100% commitment is acceptable, and that's commitment to excellence, not perfection. Nobody's perfect; we know that all too well.

Okay, if I'm 100% committed, does that mean I have to sacrifice my own happiness, independence, integrity, or choices? Good Heavens, no! Remember Rule #1: *be best friends*. Best friends are not a burden to each other. A best friend enhances your life, helps you to find happiness, and encourages your independence, integrity, and choice.

When you are all-in and fully committed, your partner's happiness, independence, integrity, and choices are important to you. Their happiness is your goal; their happiness is your happiness. Be encouraging; be helpful; talk to him or her about their wishes, dreams, and desires.

Conversely, unless *you* are also happy, you certainly won't be much fun to be around. Therefore, your happiness is imperative in fulfilling your partner's happiness—it's vital. A relationship is not one-sided, self-centered, instant gratification. Talk to each other and communicate about one another's wishes, dreams, and desires. With any luck and total commitment, these can become mutually achievable goals.

Okay, you might be thinking there must still be *some* sacrifice. Maybe...but let's call it *compromise* instead.

For instance, your partner will probably ask you to perform some tasks that you maybe would rather not do. However, if you learn to look at it in a different light, and realize that finishing a 'honey-do' task, or tagging along for an event that you'd rather skip will greatly please him or her, then the sacrifice ... um ... rather ... compromise no longer feels so horrible. Take pleasure in a simple smile and a thank you. This is all-in, 100% commitment.

Bird's-Eye View

All-in, 100% commitment means having restraint. Look at the big picture before you snap. Comfort your partner when he or she makes an error, instead of criticizing. Bite your lip; learn to understand that negative criticism has no material value. In other words, you can't change the past, so don't fret over it.

Is there a lesson to be learned after the error? Maybe. If so, calmly discuss better options with your partner after the smoke has cleared and each of you has had some time to cool off. Be a comforting and consoling friend. Is it tough? Oh, you bet! But with practice, you will get better at it—better, not perfect. This is a big picture thing.

Compliment him when he finishes the honey-do task. And remember, unless you are joking and have that type of relationship, this is NOT the time to say, "Well, it's about time!" Again, talk things over calmly when you disagree; admit when you are wrong; be the peace maker, or better yet, the peace keeper.

This may seem difficult, and yes it is! It takes a lot of practice, and sometimes your tongue will bleed from biting it so hard, but all-in means you are going to work *friggin'* hard at these principles and the remainder of the 15 Rules. Moments of anger, jealousy, and an inflated ego can create lasting damage to a relationship. Think wisely and carefully before reacting. Hurtful words can leave open wounds and scars that sometimes never heal. Walk away if it helps to avoid a 'situation.' And practice, practice, practice. This is all-in, 100% commitment to a loving, lasting, and satisfying relationship.

CHAPTER 4

Rule #3
Don't Sweat the Small Stuff

"Nothing in the affairs of men is worthy of great anxiety."

~ Plato ~
Greek Philosopher
427 - 347 BC

My twice-divorced Dad lived with us for several years leading up to his passing. Always willing to help others in need, Janet and I were glad to help him with a place to stay in the hopes that his health would improve, and he'd be able to live on his own again. We did this in spite of having tough financial times, because love outweighs everything else.

We also tried to do our best to have fun as a family. For instance, snow skiing was often only possible by bargain-hunting ski equipment, skiing at night because it was cheaper, and penny-pinching wherever and whenever possible.

One place to penny-pinch was at the grocery store. We often shared or took turns grocery shopping. During one of Janet's shopping adventures, she discovered quite a deal on cat food. Janet described this opportunity as a deal she couldn't pass up. It was such a good deal; she bought *lots* of these cans of cat food.

A Bad Cat-titude

Now let me back up a bit and tell you about our one-and-only house cat, AJ. To put it lightly, AJ was a finicky eater. She would literally turn her nose up like a snobbish aristocrat to anything that wasn't her preferred brand, flavor, *and* texture—it had to be mushy.

Janet, knowing the cat's snobbish palate, but thinking she could outsmart it, purchased this bargain cat food because it was the same brand and flavor, but was chunky instead of mushy. Janet later said, "I thought I'd just 'smush' the chunks with a fork until they became mushy, and then the cat wouldn't know the difference."

Well, the cat wasn't fooled one bit and started a hunger strike—apparently protesting Janet's callous attempt at feline deception.

My father, being sympathetic to the cat's plight, became angry at Janet's 'insensitivity' towards the cat's mushy food preference.

Downstairs in the basement, I was tinkering with a motorcycle, completely unaware of the cat's plight and the escalating dispute between my Dad, Janet, and AJ. However, I was quickly brought up to speed by my now excited father regarding the cat's hunger strike.

"Aren't you going to do something about this?" he exclaimed. "Are you just going to take it? You need to speak up!"

I took a moment to weigh the gravity of the situation, and then I calmly replied, "Dad, you cooked dinner when I lived with you. What would you have done if I refused to eat it?"

"Well, you'd go hungry," he quickly replied.

"Yes, exactly," I responded. "And if our kids didn't like what we cooked, they'd go hungry too. Why is the cat any different?"

In a huff, Dad stormed off.

In the end, the cat got her mushy food after my wife's very next trip to the store and survived her hunger strike to go on with her pretentious ways!

This whole episode could have easily blown up. I could have blamed Janet for being so insensitive towards the cat's food preference, and she could have blamed me for, well, lots of things. The point is, we both weighed the magnitude of the complaints and realized, looking at the big picture, that this was not a big deal.

This, of course, is just one small example in any number of scenarios that might have been blown way out of proportion on any given day in a relationship. Work, kids, financial challenges, time-management, relatives, etc. are all possible stressors and an opportunity for disagreement.

As we discussed in Rule #2, moments of anger, jealousy, and an inflated ego can cause lasting damage to a relationship. Words hurt, sometimes more than anything else. Think wisely and carefully before reacting.

Janet was well-intentioned and meant no harm to the family cat. She was only trying to make ends meet during a difficult financial time. I was wise to understand this. I was also careful to keep a cool head, even when being provoked to do the opposite.

We suggest that every time an opportunity for dispute arises, you weigh the importance of the situation in the context of your relationship. When considered in this light, most, if not all, disagreements and differences become small stuff.

On the other hand, if you are doing something that is irritating your partner, please stop. For instance:

- Take out the trash when the can is full.
- Fold the clothes.
- Put gas in the car when you take it.
- Place your underwear in the hamper, not on the floor.
- Use a coaster under your drinking glass.
- Cover your mouth when you cough or sneeze.
- Good grief, make the bed in the morning.
- Oh, and the biggie: Rinse your dish *thoroughly* before putting it in the dishwasher.

Now, the latter may seem irrational to some of you. After all, isn't a dishwasher designed to rinse the dishes for you? Yes, but we've already established that best friends accept each other's quirks, so if this small thing makes your 'quirky' friend happy, *then do it!*

We can honestly say that because of this philosophy and our practice of it, we've been deprived of make-up sex. Never had it. Why? Because neither one of us sweats the small stuff.

CHAPTER 5

Rule #4
Compliment

"A simple, I love you, means more than money."

~ Frank Sinatra ~
American Singer
1915-1998

Steve and I have had the pleasure of attending many seminars on leadership strategies. One recurring theme for effective leadership is the human need for praise, compliments, and recognition for a job well done. In most, if not all, employee satisfaction surveys, this need consistently ranks well above even a person's rate of pay as a motivational factor and can be the reason why someone stays at or leaves a job. Perhaps this recognition (or lack thereof) is a factor in your career.

Maybe this praise is something lacking in your relationship, as well. Our suggestion is to start—lead by example—give praise, recognition, or thanks to your partner, and do it often. Say it with conviction, with a warm smile and a glimmer in your eyes. Try it; it's not hard, really. With practice, you'll get better. Most importantly, your partner will feel liked, loved, and appreciated, and perhaps will compliment you in return. It's a win-win and a Rule to achieving relationship happiness.

Many years ago, one of my friends remarked that Steve "had potential." To this day, I'm not sure if this was a backhanded compliment or whether she was being genuine. Either way, she did a very skillful job at spinning a positive message. We encourage you to try the same approach.

Might you be saying, "Compliment him? He's got a huge beer belly, an oversized bald head, and more hair than Sasquatch on the rest of his body. How on earth can I compliment someone who resembles an orangutan?"

Or, you may be thinking, "Compliment her? But she is..." well, no, on second thought, we are not going there. But you get the point.

Nonetheless, even though he may resemble a Yeti, we might be able to assume that perhaps he has a nice smile and shows *some* intelligence. Try complimenting his smile, his intelligence, or any other good trait. Those good things *are* there if you look hard. You probably don't have to look far if you put on a set of rose-colored glasses and set aside any negativity.

If you are having real difficulty, try a simple, "I appreciate you," or "Thank you for being my friend." Practice, practice, practice. What do you have to lose?

Relationships are not give-and-take; they are give-and-get. You can't expect to be loved if you don't give love. You can't expect to get compliments if you don't give compliments. You can't expect a friendship if you aren't a friend.

But it goes even further. Loving and caring for someone and being a friend is only meaningful, only *possible*, when you love, and more importantly, like yourself. Take care of yourself emotionally and physically; be positive and encouraging. It's okay; loving and liking yourself is not egotistical or narcissistic. However, it is a must if you truly want to be a valued friend. This self-care is not negotiable, loving and liking yourself is vital for you to be able to give love to others.

Taking care of your relationship by taking care of yourself takes some discipline. For example, during your relationship, you and your partner are going to age, get wrinkles, and sag. You lose or even gain hair in weird places. Or sometimes you gain weight because of unforeseen circumstances, a sedentary job, or after the birth of a child. We know the latter from experience; we *both* gained weight after our first child. I craved pickles and hot fudge sundaes (a lot of them!) and Steve, out of 'loyal support,' had just as many hot fudge sundaes as I did.

Circumstances like these are understandable. I can't claim that we genuinely eat healthy or exercise regularly, but doing your best to watch your health *and* personal hygiene is being respectful to your partner.

Watching your mental health, at least what is within your control, is also essential for a healthy relationship. Again, life happens, and sometimes mental health issues can strike without warning, but we would argue that you at least have *some* control over your destiny.

When our adult daughter was killed in a motorcycle accident, it was a devastating blow to both of us and our family. What we learned is, no matter how hard one tries to understand the impact such tragedy has on their mental health, it is impossible to fathom unless it happens to them. Shock doesn't even begin to describe the feeling. The mind races uncontrollably for days, weeks, and months over "what-ifs" and "if-onlys." Words cannot describe the magnitude of regret, sorrow, anguish, depression, and anxiety that weighs heavily on your heart and mind, and how these emotions can continue to haunt you for years, perhaps a lifetime, after a devastating loss.

We both experienced these emotions at the magnitude and for the length of time we just described. It would have been far easier for either one of us to give up on living than it was to pick ourselves up by the bootstraps. Sucking it up was utterly exhausting, but we did because not doing so would have been, in a sense, selfish and uncaring. It would have meant giving up on ourselves and giving up on our partner, too. We don't want to sound insensitive, but this is a real example of our daily fight, our struggle to overcome darkness when it would have been much easier to let depression consume one or both of us.

You may be in a struggle of your own. We fully understand that these hardships can be all-consuming and crippling. Seek help and seek happiness. Take care of yourself so that you can take care of your relationship.

Happiness and optimism are not feelings that come to you as "*Magic rays of sunshine that come down when you're feelin' blue*" (*The Waterboy*, 1998, Touchtone Pictures). Happiness and optimism start and resonate from inside of you. These feelings are contagious. Focus on your well-being, then be positive, loving, compliment often and be sure to say 'those three words' like you mean them. Say *I love you*, with a smile and that twinkle in your eye. In so doing, you 'infect' your partner.

CHAPTER 6
Rule #5
Admit When You Are Wrong

"It ain't the heat; it's the humility."

~ Yogi Berra ~
New York Yankees player, manager, and coach
1925 - 2015

"I'd be the first to admit when I'm wrong. I've never been wrong. But if I ever was ..." Do you know anyone like that?

Let's face it; admitting you are wrong is extremely difficult. You literally feel resistance deep down, in your chest, shoulders, back of your head, and undoubtedly in your throat. Then, if you make it past all that, your brain dumbs you down as it continues to block your confession at your mouth. You stutter, even though you never stuttered before. "I waahh...szz ... wr... wr...ong." It's animalistic, almost like a caveman's survival depended on never admitting fault.

Regardless, there may be a time... or two... or three... where you realize that you were wrong about an idea, person, or paint color. Love, in this case, is humility. Admit you were wrong and give credit to your partner for the win. Additionally, don't forget to say those three important words in a relationship: *I am sorry.* Yes, those three words, followed by the other three words: *I love you.* Hopefully, the latter helps to smooth things over, although we offer no guarantees.

Once again, this humility takes great restraint and control. It's not easy to swallow your ego and fess up. After all, we all love to be correct all the time. Admitting you were wrong is admitting you have faults. And let's be honest; admitting you have flaws is painful.

But not everything is about just you. Admitting fault is about your team, your relationship. Showing humility is showing love, friendship, and trust. In other words, through humility, you are demonstrating a strong, ethical character, which will help to build a more trusting relationship.

On the flip side, for the person in the right, an apology is an excellent opportunity for smiles and a laugh, not resentment or an "I told you so." Support and encourage your best friend— always. Anger and resentment over honest mistakes have no value and are damaging to a relationship. Forgive errors that were otherwise well-intended.

Look at mistakes as a valuable education, even when they are costly. As someone once told us after an expensive error, "Well, you got educated, and everyone knows education is expensive." Live and learn. More on *that* topic later.

CHAPTER 7

Rule #6

You Don't Have to Win an Argument (Even When You Are Right)

"Choose your battles wisely. After all, life isn't measured by how many times you stood up to fight. It's not winning battles that makes you happy, but it's how many times you turned away and chose to look in a better direction…."

~ C. JoyBell C. ~
American Author

J anet and I bet you know at least one person with whom it is simply not worth debating. You know, the one who thinks a debate or a disagreement is a *take no prisoners, winner take all, duel to the death*. Let's hope this person is *not* your current partner.

If you are in a relationship, you will inevitably have a difference of opinion. It's going to happen. For example, there certainly are going to be opportunities for disagreement in areas of dinner choices, financial goals, home remodeling ideas, and, of course, the big one—children—just to name just a few. However, the goal is to have a *debate* and avoid a *fight.* Your role in this situation is to focus on de-escalation, to circumvent a nonproductive, relationship damaging battle.

Jean and Rex, married forty-three years, described this technique as the "art of arguing without fighting," where each person continuously strives to "keep it scaled down … knowing that, in the end, we are on the same team."

Won the Battle, but Lost the War

Ok, so you and your partner are in a disagreement about something. Perhaps one partner forgot to do something he or she promised to do, or her honey-do list doesn't match up with his. Perhaps one of the kids needs to be taught a lesson for a wrongdoing, and the partners disagree as to the length and type of lesson it should be. Or, perhaps one of you ruined dinner. There are probably hundreds of scenarios that could occur, and in any given relationship they do.

Ah, but this scenario is where negotiation skills, or better yet, the willingness to compromise, become tantamount to avoiding the war. Too often, we've witnessed others (e.g., family, friends) completely blow up and go at each other over what sometimes seems to us to be a minor issue. You've likely witnessed the same. Remember Rule #3 - *Don't Sweat the Small Stuff.*

Before immediately debating with your partner over a difference of opinion, first ask yourself, "What do I have to gain by winning this argument?" Oftentimes, winning becomes an ego thing, with no real value. Winning an argument, getting your way, or getting your point across while doing damage to your relationship is winning the battle, but losing the war.

We know this advice is going to sound daunting, but a healthy relationship requires that you and your partner think *big picture* on a daily, even hourly basis. Your relationship is at a risk if you choose a *take no prisoners, winner take all, duel to the death* approach to most disagreements. Breathe, listen to your partner's perspective, weigh the options, keep calm, rationalize, negotiate, swallow your pride, and perhaps do some compromising, even when you *know* you are right. Remember, don't sweat the small stuff. Is it worth the fight?

"I've Got a Snaking Suspicion"

Over the past summer, we had some unwanted guests camping out under the stone steps going up to the front door of our home. We first discovered these interlopers when our mail carrier stated to Janet, perhaps jokingly, that she was no longer going to deliver packages to the front door because she was deathly afraid of the snakes sunning themselves there. Thanks to that mail carrier, I now had a new honey-do task added to my ever-growing list.

The next day, I was home early enough to investigate the claim, and sure enough, there they were: two snakes perched on one of the large stone steps. Janet immediately ordered their relocation.

Before you get all coiled up, start hissing, or freak out the way the mail carrier and Janet did, it is important to note that no UPS or FedEx carriers lodged any formal complaints. It is also important to note that, in Massachusetts, venomous snakes are rare. In fact, of the 14 species of snakes in Massachusetts, the only venomous types are the Northern Copperhead and the Timber Rattlesnake. Each one of these is *so rare* they are protected by the Massachusetts Endangered Species Act (Audubon, 2019). Having been assigned several snake-removal demands in the past, I was already aware of these venomous snake facts.

To uncoil this situation, my investigation revealed that the snakes were small, only one or two feet in length and simply of the common Garter Snake variety, which during the warm months can be seen often and everywhere.

Having a warm heart, I chose to take a more passive approach that would make any Greenpeace activist proud. I simply let the snakes be, as I saw no harm with them living there. I did comment to Janet that perhaps "snakes" should be added to the US Postal Service motto that "neither wind, nor rain, nor snow … stays these couriers from the swift completion of their appointed rounds."

Thankfully, as summer progressed and fall approached, our guests appeared to have moved on. That is, until one day while I was working on a project in the basement, I got the uneasy feeling that I was being watched. Sure enough, above me, on top of the foundation, I discovered a snake. I looked carefully at my slithering friend to make sure it was, in fact, a friendly sort of a snake, and then I tried to grab it to relocate it. However, before I could grab it, the thing got away; apparently he went somewhere in the wall. I asked myself, "How do I get rid of the snake without causing a panic?" I answered myself, "First, DO NOT TELL JANET!" Then I figured I'd do some internet research, when I had some spare time.

With all my careful planning, I made one crucial mistake. I told our Granddaughter Kaylyn, who I thought was a trusted confidante, about the house guest. BIG MISTAKE! At the first opportunity, that 'snake in the grass' spilled the beans to Janet in the car. As I could have predicted, panic ensued, and more importantly for this chapter, so did an immediate and heated telephone debate as to how quickly this snake was going to be 'relocated.'

In her panic, caused by a terrible and unjust fear of snakes (or at least that's how I saw it), Janet seemingly forgot about Rules two through six. Or, was it, perhaps, that in her haste (or justified concern—that's still up for debate) she felt I was less than honest in our supposed 100% all-in relationship? Then again, maybe she was entirely justified in *sweating* what I perceived as *small stuff*. In my defense, the snake *was* very small. Nonetheless, to my surprise, she couldn't conjure up even one *compliment* when I mentioned this to her. Maybe, Janet was convinced that snake infestation voids the *you don't have to win an argument* Rule, or she was certain she was entirely right, I was wrong, and it was time for me to *admit I was wrong*, or all the above.

Before we continue, let's be fair to Janet. In hindsight, and because I was so acutely aware of Janet's phobia, I should have moved more quickly to evict those slithering creatures, and I do admit that I certainly didn't foresee them moving inside when the weather got cooler—an honest mistake. Well, unless you know anything about snakes, which I clearly don't. Finally, I should not have shared the news with our "can't keep a secret" granddaughter! I was wrong, period. End of story. Okay, it's really not the end of the story, but now that I've cleared that up and 'set the stage,' we can continue.

Here we had the perfect ingredients for an all-out blow-up, resentment, and permanent relationship damage, and it got heated for a bit—actually much longer than a bit—but cooler heads eventually prevailed. After some exciting words, time to ourselves (she was still driving, and I refused to discuss it over the phone) we agreed that same evening to an expedited plan to eradicate the unwanted serpent.

Throughout all this panic and this heated debate, I could have gotten defensive, but instead I admitted my misjudgment of snake behavior and humbly agreed to a joint ...er ...Janet's expedited eradication plan.

Janet had an excellent opportunity to find fault, get angry, and hold a grudge, but instead she decided to forgive and forget. Each of us carefully chose our words as we discussed the plan. No harm, no foul. We eventually paid each other some compliments, and luckily we have not seen any snakes in a while. Then again, if the snake does return, we will have to amend this chapter in another book.

We know that all disagreements can't and won't be solved this easily, but your goal should always be for a quick, painless solution—one that preserves your relationship. Be fair, be kind, and be calm. Be cognizant of your behavior and your words, and bite your lip until you are truly ready to have a respectful debate.

Focus on one disagreement at a time, and *do not* bring up past issues or arguments which should have been settled already *and forgotten*. Avoid statements like:

"Every time I …, you …"

"You never …"

"You always …"

"Last time you …"

You might be thinking, "WTF, that's gonna be tough." Yes, it is. But remember, practice, practice, practice. It's all about the big picture: preserving your relationship by controlling your emotions and words, until you can think rationally and communicate calmly.

The longer you let the disagreement fester, the more likely long-term grudges and bad feelings are to take hold. It's best to take time to settle differences in the moment, no matter how difficult.

We don't recommend it, but in those rare cases where you absolutely cannot come to an accord due to unforeseen circumstances, *respectfully* agree to table the matter until a later time. Agree on a specific time and keep it. Do not hope your partner will forget about it; he or she will not.

Respecting your partner means that you take any grievance seriously. Try to settle all differences and come to some conclusion, compromise, or agreement before going to sleep.

Having a snake in the house was a very serious matter to Janet, as it probably would be for a lot of you reading this. She demanded and expected a determined plan to eradicate the snake. Most importantly, it was a joint plan that we agreed to that very night. It was a quick solution when I finally (after the snake moved into the house) took her grievance seriously. I listened; therefore we avoided grudges and bad feelings.

During any disagreement, to avoid long-term relationship damage, it's important to always remember:

- Look at the big picture.
- We're on the same team.
- We are best friends.
- Pay each other compliments.
- Smile and laugh.
- Don't sweat the small stuff.
- Forgive and forget.
- Practice humility.

CHAPTER 8
Rule #7
Don't Blame

"Blame keeps wounds open. Only forgiveness heals."

~ Thomas S. Monson ~
American Religious Leader
1927 - 2018

"You always …"

"I told you so …"

"You never …"

"I knew this would happen …"

"It's all your fault …"

"I blame you …"

"You should have gotten rid of those snakes a long time ago …."

Blame is one of a few emotions that have no material or spiritual value. It's ugly, and it tears at the very soul of the person harboring resentment.

We get it; depending on the harm done, forgiveness can be extremely tough. Was the hurt intentional, or was it unintentional? Was it a calculated wrong (e.g., infidelity), or was it an accident?

Indeed, in all relationships, wrongdoings occur that may cause irreversible harm, or at the very least, damage trust. We want to make it clear that we are not advocating for staying in a relationship that is causing you pain, heartache, or stress. We hope to give you the tools, the Rules, and the strength to strive for a lasting relationship, but one that is both loving and satisfying. Such a relationship is not possible, of course, without a mutual understanding of the Rules, and a good, honest, personal assessment of what makes you happy and satisfied.

Throughout our relationship, there have been plenty of opportunities for blame. Without digging up painful details, those include business failure, loss of a job, a car crash (a beautiful Camaro), career choices, accidental death, losing a political campaign, and many, many more. Even though these factors could lead to the death knell for some relationships, ours remains strong.

Why and how does our relationship survive and even thrive?

Our success is due to our *best friend* and *big picture* thinking. We *are* each other's best friends. Best friends accept each other for who they are, including their faults, human fragility, and imperfections.

Always ask yourself, "What was his or her intention?" Even if you can say that your partner's scheme or action was foolish, ill-conceived, or they shoulda'-coulda'-woulda,' try to look beyond the weeds. Take a good look at your partner's—your friend's—soul; despite the outcome, was his or her intent well-meaning and intended not to cause you or another any pain? If the answer is yes, we ask you to consider forgiveness. Talk it over, find the lesson, and then move on together. If the aim was to cause deliberate harm, then you need to take a deeper dive into the nature of your relationship.

Healing Through Forgiveness

In addition to not placing blame on your partner, don't hold grudges towards others. Just like we said before, anger, resentment, jealousy, and blame only hardens the heart of the one who holds these emotions. We've both felt that 'hatred' deep down inside at one time or another, and unless you are divine, you probably have too. The feeling literally weighs heavily on your heart and in your chest, raising your blood pressure and causing you to clench your teeth. This pressure has no value other than, perhaps, a lesson to be learned. Make a note, eliminate that person from your life if need be, and move on. Learn, and then forgive. "*Trust, but verify,*" a wise man once said. Removing dark thoughts within you makes you a better, more loving person.

When you let go of the resentment, the feeling *is* divine. The weight and heaviness disappear. Remember, a grudge only hurts you. That emotion has no bearing, whatsoever, on the person at whom it is directed. Forgiveness relieves *you* of that burden, no one else.

If You're Looking for Someone to Blame, Look in the Mirror

The above sentiment is good advice, but good heavens, man (←said in a snooty, pretentious voice) while you are at it, forgive yourself. Go ahead, take the blame. You probably deserve it. Heck, we all do something stupid sometimes. But *guilt* is just another of those useless emotions if you let it linger and depress you. No one gains anything at all, not a single ounce of 'mojo,' from your guilt. Though it is possibly the hardest thing to do, forgive yourself, learn, and move on.

Letting go of negative vibes will make you a better and happier person, and, conversely, hanging on to them can damage your relationship. Learning to forgive your partner, others, and yourself is empowering. Taking care of yourself, emotionally, is your contribution to your relationship, and it is absolutely imperative to your happiness. Remember, *your* happiness is your contribution to a mutually happy relationship. That means a happy team starts with you doing your part. Forgive yourself and forgive others. Allow yourself to be happy.

CHAPTER 9
Rule #8
Have Fun

"True love doesn't happen right away; it's an ever-growing process. It develops after you've gone through many ups and downs, when you've suffered together, cried together, laughed together."

~ Ricardo Montalban ~
Actor
1920-2009

"**B**ut honey, you're not even funny," was my immediate, unfiltered response to Steve's proclamation that he signed up as a contestant in the local Toastmaster's Humorous Speech contest, after being dared to do so by two friends at a local pub. With a grin and a laugh, Steve agreed, "Yes, I know. What the hell did I get myself into?"

To some, my comment might be construed as offensive, but it wasn't to him. Yes, at that moment I failed miserably at filtering my thoughts, but we are best friends first, and friends can get away with teasing each other occasionally. We laughed because I was right. But, to my amazement, he won and won again. Huh… he *can* be funny. Who knew?

It seems too often that couples take their relationship way too seriously. Sadly, some think the intense drama you see between couples on television and in movies is normal. I'm sorry, but all that is nonsense. Yes, it happens, but drama is unhealthy if it creeps into your relationship.

We've been told that an occasional fight is good. Wrong! Fighting is not healthy communication. You need to settle disagreements without escalating to shouting. If you're shouting and fighting, you are moving far away from a fun relationship.

Get to know your partner and choose your words carefully to avoid anything hurtful. Moreover, don't EVER intentionally say something cruel. There is no room for cruelty, period.

Best friends have fun, relax, and joke together. Your goal should be to re-create the emotions you had when you were with a childhood friend—that comfort of being entirely yourself, and the easy-going, no-stress feeling you had when you were together.

Find opportunities to laugh together. We laugh while we are performing household chores, raking leaves, shoveling snow, cooking, watching a comedy, driving, and in the bedroom. We laugh and joke when it's just the two of us and when we're with family and friends.

We even manage to laugh when things don't go as planned; for example, when we make a *very* bad choice of vacation motels or a terrible choice for an ingredient in one of Steve's experimental meals.

We enjoy being together because each of us strives to make togetherness fun. It's a win-win. Lead by example; be the cheerleader. Try it! It's fun, satisfying, and makes for a much better day, or just a better moment.

A Smile is as Contagious as a Yawn

It's unexplainable, but for some strange reason, yawns are contagious. You may be feeling the urge to yawn right now just because I brought it up.

A warm, friendly, loving smile seems to have the same effect. A smile usually begets a smile in return. Combine that smile with a gentle touch or a warm hug, and you've struck gold. Well, you'll have struck gold with your welcoming partner. DON'T ever try this with a surprised stranger or co-worker. It usually has the opposite effect, or at least we think it will. We've never tried it... or at least we won't admit we have.

Relationship happiness starts with you. Be an example: smile, hug, and cuddle. Be ridiculous; be fun. Look for the humor in everyday experiences, and look even harder in tough situations. Share whatever humor you can find with your partner.

Hug him or her for no reason at all. Why? "Because I'm happy to be with you," or "You're so cute," or even just "Thank you for being here with me."

Sharing is Caring

"Hey, did you see …?"

"Did you hear …?"

"I gotta show you this..."

"You won't believe..."

Share fun stores—not negative ones—with your partner. Tell those stories with a wide, bright smile and a glimmer in your eyes. Sharing interesting and humorous stories, adventures, and misadventures with your partner demonstrates that they are quite possibly the most important person in your life, even when they can't be with you. Whether you tell it over the phone or later, in person, have fun telling each other stories about things that happen when you're apart. That's friendship, and that's caring.

Good times, Bad Times

"Okay," you might say. "So you laugh, smile, and have fun during good times, but what about bad times? How does that happen?"

We understand. Depending on the situation, sometimes it's difficult to smile and have fun. As we've discussed earlier, we know those situations all too well. However, during very serious and difficult times, regardless of their magnitude, you need to be fun to be around.

Of course, you can cry, mourn, and be sad. And you may need some time alone. But it's also very important that you support your partner by not checking out. Sure, depending on the venue and the seriousness of the bad times, others may see laughing and smiling as inappropriate, but there is fun in a warm smile, gentle touch, and a hug. Showing love and being emotionally supportive is fun, or at least uplifting, in its own unique way. Steve's compassion, support, and friendliness were my refuge during some of my seemingly unbearable times. Although he was experiencing the same grief and despair, he kept me grounded through these hard times. In turn, I focused on doing the same for him—being his oasis— which created a win-win situation.

The Bates Motel

Okay, serious issues aside, let's discuss those less serious bad times. We call them our 'stories,' and damn, we've got quite a few. But Nova Scotia might be our prime example. That day was just awful.

Years ago, Steve and I rode a motorcycle two-up around the Cabot Trail from our Massachusetts home. Two friends on separate motorcycles joined us for our adventure on this scenic and famous coastal road on Cape Breton Island at the northern tip of Nova Scotia, Canada.

We usually don't plan our overnight stops, opting most times to wing it. This late June trip was no different, and we discovered a rather large motel somewhere in a remote area of the island.

It seemed strange, but we appeared to be the only guests. Perhaps this high vacancy rate should have been a clue as to how our evening was going to go. The motel had a large, inviting swimming pool, but the water was a darker green than an evergreen tree's needles. The rooms had a damp, musty smell; each had a refrigerator, but neither worked.

No problem. We bought some ice at a local store (because the motel had none), lined one of the room's trash cans with a trash bag, and used it to keep our beer and wine chilled.

On a motorcycle trip, you don't have the luxury of carrying many clothes. As a result, we needed to wash some clothes that evening. Not surprisingly, however, there wasn't a working washer or dryer at the motel. The owner instructed us that we could do laundry at a campground a few miles away. With a large bag of dirty clothes strapped to our bike, Steve and I eagerly set out to find that campground. Our friends chose to stay behind and drink some of the wine and beer. This choice turned out to be the wiser one.

If you think mosquitoes are the worst creatures on Earth, devised from the evil mind of Satan himself, you must have never been to northern Maine or the Southeastern part of Canada in June. There, they have the nastiest blood-sucking creatures ever to walk...er...fly on this planet—the dreaded black fly. It must have been an exceptionally good year to be a black fly, too, because the air was filled with them when we arrived at the campground. "Why would anyone want to camp here?" we thought. Of course, *we* were there, too.

To start, the only washing machine at the campground didn't spin, so the clothes were drenched when we removed them. We hand-wrung them out as best we could, then threw them in the campground's only dryer, which started with a loud squeal and then barely tumbled. So, after a little of Steve's mechanical troubleshooting, we put just a few articles in, and *ta-da!* The squeal went away...mostly.

There we were, having not yet eaten dinner, sitting in a bug-infested field, waiting for impossibly wet clothes to dry, and slapping each other continuously. Well, slapping black flies on each other continuously.

We chit-chatted for quite a while until Steve noticed that he'd done a pretty piss-poor job of protecting me from these bloodsuckers. From my itching, I suspected this was the case. Long before the clothes had dried at all, Steve noticed that I looked like I had developed a terrible case of the chicken pox. Oh, it was bad! I was covered in red blotches *and* scratching like a mangy dog. Steve wasn't faring much better.

We grabbed the wet clothes from the worthless dryer and high-tailed it out of there back to the motel, planning instead to hang the clothes out to dry in the damp, musty room. We rummaged through our bags for some crackers to eat while enjoying the beer and wine; because, as it turned out, there were no open restaurants for many, many miles.

Not unexpectedly, the clothes were still quite wet the following morning. So, we bungee-strapped each piece of wet clothing onto our three respective motorcycles. Picture this: Jane and Tony traveling down the backroads of Canada on their Harley and Suzuki with our underwear and pants flapping in the breeze. This was undoubtedly a one-of-a-kind sight and something that only good friends would do. As a side-note, though, no photos exist of Jane and Tony's well-decorated motorcycles that morning, because, as they put it, "Hey, friendship has limits! We want no photos on Facebook with our bikes and your underwear!"

Oh, we laughed all night. We laughed together, we laughed with our friends while riding and drying our clothes on the motorcycles, and we *even* laughed as we slapped the black flies.

You Had the Power All Along, My Dear

You can choose your mood. You can be happy and fun, or you can be miserable. How you feel is your choice in *any* situation. Suck it up when things are going badly; put on those friggin' rose-colored glasses and live a little! Laugh a little, too, because you at least are going to have one hell of a story when the nightmare is over.

Cabot Trail, Nova Scotia, Canada

CHAPTER 10
Rule #9
Give Acceptance

"A friend is someone who gives you total freedom to be yourself – and especially to feel, or not feel. Whatever you happen to be feeling at any moment is fine with them. That's what real love amounts to – letting a person be what he really is."

~ Jim Morrison ~
American Singer
1943-1971

I know we've picked on Janet a bit, but I've been ribbed too. Remember, it's all in fun; relationships are about accepting the good and less-than-perfect traits.

They Come in Pairs

So, Janet has this thing about socks. It drives me crazy. When all the laundry has been washed, and there isn't a stitch of clothing remaining to sort through and fold, Janet insists on throwing away any sock that doesn't have a mate.

Unless you agree with Janet's clearly irrational behavior, you might be thinking (like me), "Wait, don't do that! It's almost certainly in a pant leg somewhere." Yet, I don't stand in the way. Ah, but if I do find a lone sock before her, I hide it. No harm, no foul. I accept what I view as a quirk, and Janet accepts what she sees as my irrational one sock hoarding behavior if she manages to find that hidden sock.

This is a simple example, but that is how easy acceptance can be. Remember Rule #1: *Don't sweat the small stuff.* Bite your lip, hard if that's what it takes, and move on. It's all in the name of acceptance.

I Gotta Be Me

Acceptance is also letting people be who they truly are. Too often, we've known couples where one partner felt forced to change or be less than they originally dreamed of becoming because their partner demanded or expected it. We are convinced these relationships are doomed to fail because the oppressed one will eventually feel resentment and unhappiness; *or,* the oppressor turns the one who is oppressed into someone different than the oppressor grew to love.

The latter is ironic, but we've seen it. The oppressor demands change; the one who is oppressed complies; in turn, the oppressor falls out of love because the oppressed becomes a different person. Ugh.

You often hear relationships described as give-and-take. But we don't see healthy relationships that way. We see give-and-take as one-sided; one person gives of themselves, and the other reaps the benefits. That scenario is not mutually nourishing. Good relationships are give-give or win-win. Let us explain.

One way to give-give is to *give up* control *over* your partner. Allow him or her the freedom to be authentic, and in return they *give* you love. Rejoice in their happiness and satisfaction, and unless you are with a narcissist, they'll likely return the favor, allowing *you* the freedom to be yourself. See? Give-give, win-win.

A Boy and his Toys

Steve collects, maintains, and rides antique motorcycles. Consequently, he is often in his man cave/workshop (which is decorated wall-to-wall and floor-to-ceiling with motorcycle photos and memorabilia), sitting on a stool with a tool in his hand and working on a motorcycle on a lift in front of him. In this solitude, he tinkers away while listening to an incredibly sappy music selection on his cell phone. He describes this activity as relaxing, satisfying, and even pleasurable.

Steve also likes—no, loves—searching the internet for hard-to-find antique motorcycle parts and 'barn-find' motorcycles. He's been a motorcycle guy since the day we met. This passion is part of what makes him who he is. I was well aware of his motorcycle mania when we met, and I knew what I was in for when we started dating.

Wrenching and riding motorcycles seemingly touches Steve's very soul. Who am I to take that away from him? It gives him pleasure (when he doesn't break a bone, that is), and that makes me happy too.

My understanding of Steve's love to tinker in the workshop or to ride one of his motorcycles is the very essence of acceptance, friendship, and love. Consequently, I don't stand in the way...well...most days......unless the leaves desperately need to be raked, or the lawn desperately needs mowing. In that case, negotiations start. Review *Rule #6* again, if you are confused.

If You Loved Me, You Wouldn't …

In our careers in long-term healthcare, we teach that it is important to understand that everyone, regardless of age or ability, has hopes, dreams, and desires, and these are a major factor in maintaining 'personhood.' Therefore, to destroy or to trivialize one's hopes, dreams, and desires, is to deny that someone of their personhood.

"Sounds pretty serious," you might be thinking. Well, it is, and we are confident it can make or break a relationship.

Ask yourself if you have heard or said the following:

- "You can't go out with your friends now that we are together."
- "I love him too much to allow him to ride a motorcycle. What if something happened? I can't live without him."
- "I know he or she will change once we are together."
- "We're going to have to trade that sports car in for a minivan."
- "That's a good-paying job; you can't quit."
- "Forget your foolish dreams."
- "When are you going to grow up and stop …?"

If you're not in a serious relationship yet, and you don't like who the person you are currently with is, or what his or her passion is, then he or *she ain't for you, honey*. Period. End of discussion. Move on. Sticking around isn't fair to either of you.

If you *are* in a serious relationship (like marriage), and you are unhappy with your situation, well then you got some 'splainin' to do. What did you know, and when did you know it?

All kidding aside, and not forgetting *Best Friends*, *All-in-100%*, *Don't Sweat the Small Stuff,* has your partner given you the chance to be yourself and be all you can be? Are you giving your partner the same consideration?

Full acceptance takes sacrifice and trust, but sacrifice and trust are what best friends do for each other. They accept one another for the unique person they are–quirks and all.

If you fell for your partner with (or even because of) their quirks and personality traits, are you still as supportive as you once were? We wholeheartedly hope so.

If you are not as supportive, or even worse, you are quashing their hopes, dreams, and desires, have *you* changed? Were you less than a genuine 'you' back then? Did you perhaps pretend to be someone else?

We all grow and change a little over time, hopefully for the better. But be cautious that you don't end up morphing into someone who isn't the original, down-to-the-bone 'you.' Remember, that original 'you' is the person whom your partner grew to like and love. Conversely, your partner's 'she' or 'he' is what attracted *you* in the first place. Let him or her *be* who he or she *is*. And you? Be yourself.

CHAPTER 11
Rule #10
Be Yourself

"Always be a first-rate version of yourself and not a second-rate version of someone else."

~ Judy Garland ~
American actress, singer, and dancer
1922 – 1969

One day, during a somewhat serious discussion about relationships, Steve asked a friend why she had divorced her husband a few years earlier. In her explanation, she described her ex as a good man, a good father to her two children, and someone she is still friendly with and respects. She described him as a man who didn't like to go out drinking or dancing, preferring a night at home instead. She said he worked too many hours, liked to watch television at night after work, and preferred a weekend puttering in the yard instead of going away. She went on to say that he was soft-spoken and kind and was someone who often preferred cuddling over sex.

"Oh," Steve responded, "Wait…you divorced him because he was boring and worked too much? Was he like that when you dated?"

She never answered Steve's unfiltered question.

The truth is, this friend was a wild child. She preferred going out on the town, had a thing for the bad boys, and LOVED sex—

or at least we assume so, because she told stories of her sexual adventures often and in R-rated detail.

Hmm. How in the world did this 'wild child' get hooked up and married to Mr. all-work, no-play? Was someone not genuinely his or herself during their courtship? Was one person planning to change the other? We will never know, but we do know the outcome.

Early on, Steve and I seemed to have magically stumbled upon a deeper understanding of how to effectively communicate and be comfortable together.

We first met at a high school concert. A local band, 'Clean Living,' was playing. I was 15, and Steve was 16. We started dating shortly after. Even at that young age, our relationship was open and honest. We felt relaxed and could be ourselves when we were together. Consequently, we became good friends.

We would sit in a field or on a stone wall for hours, discussing good and bad experiences from our past and our separate life plans—never thinking that our plans would ever include the two of us being together permanently. We would talk about our philosophies and beliefs about life and the afterlife. Sometimes we talked about nothing specific at all. We could have fun, smile, and laugh—never taking ourselves too seriously.

We quickly became best friends, enjoying even the simplest pleasures, just because we were experiencing them together. When we were apart, things were less enjoyable.

Although we spent a lot of time together, neither of us abandoned our high school friends. Each of us became another part of each other's groups. When we were with family, it was pretty much the same thing.

Yes, we were *so* young, but it turns out we were *relationship wise*. We established good, substantive communication early on, and being a friend to one another had become paramount to the relationship. We avoided silly, 'serious lover' communication like in a movie scene where the two lovers say things like:

"I love you."

"I love you more."

"Oh, take me, take me, please."

Blah, blah, blah.

Sappy, yes, but you get the picture. In that scenario, no real, serious communication is going on. Some relationships actually resemble that.

"Come on," you might be saying. "There's no way that really happens." But we have seen couples that speak and act almost as silly as these examples. Let's hope those same couples have better communication skills when they are alone.

Early in our friendship, we set the stage for a lasting relationship. We both remember one beautiful, sunny, warm afternoon that first summer vividly. We were sitting cross-legged in Steve's backyard, laughing and talking, when a young boy around three or four years old wandered over from next door. We didn't know this kid, but he was sweet, friendly, had an infectious smile, and was overly talkative. He wore a striped button-up shirt and had oversized, black-rimmed glasses that didn't seem to fit him too well, because as he spoke he would often push his glasses back up his nose closer to his face. We learned from him that his family was visiting from out of state.

Keep in mind, we were just young teens having a fun, playful discussion with this over-talkative kid. But we surmised that our children might look and act like this little guy who crossed our path.

On that day, we became close friends who established a strong trust where we didn't 'measure' the other. We could relax, let our guard down, and be ourselves.

We didn't know it at the time, but all those times we spent innocently discussing our past and our future—our pain, faults, hopes, dreams, and desires—we were brilliantly laying out the foundation for a loving, lasting, and satisfying relationship. That is, we discovered how to communicate effectively and openly, which led to learning a great deal about each other, including laying out all our 'baggage' for the other to see.

In the years to follow, we had our ups-and-downs, did some dumb stuff, sometimes wrongly hurt one or the other, and we laughed and cried. Eventually, we married—not because we had to, but because we wanted to—believing we had each found the love of our lives.

Being yourself from the start, honestly presenting who you are on the inside, faults and all, is the foundation for a strong relationship. Your relationship must start with openness and honesty. There is no substitute.

Also, at the risk of repeating, remember that your long-term happiness is dependent on your partner's happiness. Happiness is contagious.

Imagine your surprise, your disappointment, your resentment, if you were to wake up one day to realize the person you'd let into your heart, your friend, your love, and your partner, is not who you thought they were, or who they professed to be. Now, reverse the situation. Would it be fair for you to fool someone because, for whatever reason, you didn't want to or didn't feel comfortable being yourself?

From the start, be honest about your hopes, dreams, and desires, and be honest about your values. These four principles are probably the most difficult to compromise. Be sure all aspects of these four principles are out on the table before committing to a long-term relationship. It will save a lot of misunderstanding and heartache later.

Finally, don't confuse *being yourself* with being self-centered. If you are the latter, then you are not following *The Rules*. Remember, it's a balance: a win-win approach.

CHAPTER 12
Rule #11
Share Interests

"You've got to go out on a limb sometimes because that's where the fruit is."

~ Will Rogers ~
American actor, performer, humorist, and social
commentator
1879-1935

"**I** want to climb Mount Washington," Janet blurted out for no apparent reason. More intently, she asked, "Did you hear me? I think *we* should climb Mount Washington."

This certainly was an odd thing for someone who had never been a hiker or a climber to say, and it's not like I was either of those things myself. Moreover, a Mount Washington climb isn't for the faint of heart; it is certainly no easy feat.

Located in Northern New Hampshire, close to the Maine border at the northern end of the Appalachian Mountain chain, Mount Washington is the highest peak in the Northeast United States, with an elevation of 6,288 ft (1,916 m) and a vertical climb of 4,280 feet (1,300 m). It's famous for having some of the nastiest weather in the world. Until 1996, Mount Washington held the world record for the highest measured wind speed on the surface of the planet: 231 miles per hour (371.7 kph) recorded in 1934 (mountwashington.org).

"And, I want to do it on my birthday," she exclaimed.

I'll admit that I did not meet Janet's crazy, spur-of-the-moment idea with great enthusiasm. To be truthful, I hated...er... wasn't very fond of the idea. "Why hike, when you can drive to the top?" I might have asked myself back then. But, if that was what Janet wanted then, dammit, I'd do it.

Was it what I expected? NO! It was even harder—but wow! We made it up and down in 9.5 hours, certainly not even close to a record; however, it was something incredible we accomplished together.

So it began: what we now call our 'birthday challenge.' Each year, on or near our respective birthdays, we each choose an adventure and challenge the other to join in.

Together, we learned to kayak and later to navigate them in the seas. We attended several motorcycle trainings and later rode on numerous long-distance motorcycle trips on the East, South, and West coasts and almost everywhere in between. We learned to sail. We went snow skiing in spectacular places and skied some nutty trails. Enthusiastically, we attended mogul and powder skiing camps. At least, I was enthusiastic. We zip-lined across and down a mountain, rode in a hot-air balloon over the Arizona desert, and flew in a helicopter over and into the Grand Canyon. We stumbled across a black bear while we were wilderness camping. Together, we jet-skied, dirt biked, snowmobiled, mountain biked, skinny-dipped, went antiquing, and canoed with alligators. Janet reeled in a *massive* fish while deep-sea fishing and almost got vomited on while parasailing. We hiked parts of the famous Appalachian Trail and climbed other mountains, too.

Some of these things we still do and some we only did once. We don't always do everything together, but we sincerely cherish these together moments, even when it isn't something that was initially on our bucket list. Moreover, these challenges, for both of us, have helped us get over specific fears or wrong expectations, and have helped us to grow individually and as partners.

We encourage you to look for opportunities to discover shared interests. Avoid 'creepy' or uncomfortable challenges; we don't recommend that. Also, allow your partner the power to 'pass' on a challenge. However, be open-minded to a challenge, even if it's something that scares you or wasn't on your bucket list.

I went skydiving; Janet passed, but came to watch and support. Janet went hang-gliding, and well, I didn't pass, I was just too chubby to fly.

What we found is that when you try something you didn't think you would like, you may be surprised. Janet was terrified of water, but to her surprise, she found kayaking and sailing to be fun. To my surprise, I began to enjoy hiking. Yes, I really did. I'm serious.

Now, these examples of shared interests are pretty high-level, but you can find opportunities every day. Show interest in your partner's hobby, television show, work, goals, etc. Be in the present.

"How was work today?"

"Who won the football game?"

"How is that project coming along?"

Explore, search, experiment, take risks, be open-minded, and be creative as you develop common interests that are fun, exciting, and rewarding for both of you. Friendship and love are a commitment of the heart, but also a commitment of time. Be friendly, fun, and loving, and invest time in and with each other.

CHAPTER 13
Rule #12
Listen

"A significant part of showing respect is simply listening. We offer our presence and open ears—listening to the hidden hurts and heartaches, the deepest dreams and desires of one another."

~ Rick Warren ~
American pastor and author

Years ago, Steve was in Boston attending an intense Emergency Management Training, where he learned how to communicate to the public during major emergencies and disasters. The trainer explained that, before getting into any details whatsoever of what occurred or next steps, it is vitally essential for the person addressing the concerned public to start with a short comment about how they as an individual and the organization as a whole understands and is sympathetic to the public's plight. The reason for this approach is that most people will not be attuned to the speaker unless they feel the speaker has heard their concern(s). Human beings need a sympathetic ear.

Well-trained politicians use this ploy...er...technique quite often. President Clinton comes to mind with his phrase, "I feel your pain." The public loved it. He was skilled at displaying sympathy, which helped to calm an otherwise tense situation.

Similarly, good leaders use a technique called 'active listening.' To be an active listener, you stop what you are doing, make eye contact with whomever is speaking, and when appropriate, in the form of a question, paraphrase what you believe to be the concern. For example, "So, I think what you are saying is (fill in the blank). Am I correct?" This approach demonstrates active listening and indicates that you have honestly heard the other person's concern.

In your relationship, you should also be an active listener. Stop what you are doing, use eye contact, and truly listen. Repeat back for clarification.

If the discussion is regarding a difference of opinion, then settle the dispute with a civil conversation like we discussed in *Rule #5, You Don't Have to Win an Argument*.

If the conversation is about your partner's wish, desire, or a honey-do, listening is likely going to involve discussing a timeline of completion. Otherwise, you're going to have to give a *pretty good* explanation as to why you think it is isn't a good idea, or why you can't complete it now—or ever. Either way, at least your behavior shows you are *listening.*

Being a friend to your partner means that you don't discount anything you hear from him or her. For instance, I was hell-bent on climbing Mount Washington *with* Steve. He listened, meaning he acknowledged his understanding of my desire. Then, in our all-in relationship, Steve simply did what it took to get prepared to climb the mountain. If it's important to your partner, then it needs to be important to you.

Throughout this book, we emphasize the importance of communication in your relationship. Remember, the goal is not just talking to each other, the goal is *quality* communication. Genuinely listening is critical, because relationships are a two-way street. Be receptive to what your partner is telling you. Learn what his or her dreams and desires are, pay close attention to likes and dislikes, and be a listening, caring person when your partner is hurting. Be their light, and be in the moment. Sometimes a caring, sympathetic ear is all someone needs.

Dreams and desires, likes and dislikes, can, and do, change and evolve. Be receptive to new desires, visions, or concerns by actively listening daily. Share in your partner's vision and acknowledge their concerns. In other words, be a friend.

CHAPTER 14
Rule #13
Overcome Jealousy

"Jealousy is a disease, love is a healthy condition. The immature mind often mistakes one for the other, or assumes that the greater the love, the greater the jealousy — in fact, they are almost incompatible; one emotion hardly leaves room for the other."

~ Robert A. Heinlein ~
American Author
1907 - 1988

Janet and I have seen and experienced several forms of jealousy over the years. Jealousy is another of those animalistic emotions that can surface almost uncontrollably and can be ugly and damaging to your relationship if not regulated.

First, there's the jealousy towards a partner who has a better job or earns more money. Some may say, "No, that's ridiculous; how could I be jealous of my partner's career?" This may not happen to all couples; however, be cautious because it can and does occur.

If you begin to feel this emotion take hold, fight it; after all, you are a team. Be happy for your partner. Moreover, if you are dissatisfied with your situation or your career, look at your partner's success as an opportunity for you to switch careers, start or finish school, or start that side business. We've used this principle of teamwork to better our *joint* income and improve our happiness.

In our children's preschool years, Janet was a stay-at-home mom. We were both grateful to be allowed this opportunity. During this same time, she started a daycare business at our home, which was a win-win. She was able to stay home to support our kids during their very formative years, while beginning a foray into what became our introduction to the world of small business ownership.

When the kids started school, Janet turned her attention to earning a college degree in nursing, capping off a goal she had held since childhood.

With Janet firmly settled as an RN, we started a full-time business. When the opportunity arose, I began and completed a college degree in healthcare management. When I was firmly settled in with a position as a Nursing Home Administrator, Janet felt comfortable enough to make what she viewed as a risky career move.

Everything we accomplished and every step we took, we saw as a team effort. Instead of feeling resentment or jealousy, we used our good fortune to better each other.

Maybe you are seeing or wishing for an opportunity. Talk about your thoughts with your partner. Be a team. Nothing is guaranteed, and change is always difficult. But if things do work out, it's a win-win.

Skiing is Believing

Many years ago, I had gotten out of shape after focusing more on a new business venture than on my health or fitness. Janet, on the other hand, was in exceptionally good shape, and after I taught her how to ski several years earlier, started skiing with a friend when I couldn't go.

She would come back excited, with elaborate stories about skiing challenging, expert-only, trails all day.

I wasn't jealous of the time she had with her friend, but I was quickly jealous of Janet's talent and physical stamina when I joined her skiing one day. I was way too out of shape to ski at her level and speed. I quickly got out of breath, my legs started burning early, and I fell a lot.

I was so bad that my jealousy later turned to sympathy, because poor Janet lost out on a good day of skiing by having to spend most of the day waiting for me. It was embarrassing.

Going back to Rule #11: *Shared Interests*, sometimes it takes dedication and hard work to share an interest. I could have easily given up skiing that day, but I couldn't and didn't because it was something Janet loved to do. I loved her too much to let her down.

It was a tough winter, but I slowly got better. My stamina improved, and consequently my skills improved. An ugly emotion transformed into personal motivation, making me a better ski partner for Janet.

In these two areas, we have examples of situations where jealousy could have severely damaged our relationship, yet it didn't. Why? Because it goes back to being *best friends* first. Genuinely best friends aren't resentful and don't give up on each other. More importantly, they support each other and stay committed to their relationship.

Now, let's get to the biggie, and the ugliest of all, jealousy of the heart. Without a doubt, jealousy of the heart tears at the soul, and often is the most difficult to control.

Janet and I will admit that we've both harbored this ugly emotion on one or more occasions. Yet, as we've grown older, trust and maturity have overtaken youthful pettiness.

In our early years together, the emotion was much stronger simply because we didn't enjoy the trust and respect that we have for each other now. Moreover, having both been raised in families where lack of trust and infidelity were a reality, we had a deep-rooted mistrust of the institution of marriage and harbored insecurities typically inherent in one's younger years and early on in any relationship.

A jealous person begins to look at their partner as a 'catch' and 'property.' I will be the first to admit that I had a tough time with this emotion early in our marriage and found it difficult to keep in check.

On one occasion, my emotion boiled over, and I lashed out at Janet. I vividly remember and regret taking her off a club dance floor because she was dancing with another man. Jealousy overpowered me, and I was unable to think clearly. It was what can best be described as a jealous rage. In that instance, jealousy overtook me, and a split second later my emotions had moved from calm to enraged.

Janet and I are sure this early jealousy was derived from insecurities we both harbored. To better explain, early on in your relationship, even if you are already married, you don't have the years of experience together. Building trust takes time, but it also takes time to build confidence in oneself.

I admit that early on I lacked self-confidence and didn't see myself as Janet saw me. Although she viewed me as her loyal best friend and someone she wished to spend the rest of her life with, I was concerned that she would wise up someday and find someone better. This insecurity was undoubtedly at the root of my early jealousy.

At the very same time, a much younger Janet had two small children at home, and I was realistically the only breadwinner. Back then, Janet saw herself as having no marketable skills. Looking back, Janet describes her jealousy as more of a survival instinct. In other words, she and our children's survival depended on me staying loyal to my duty to provide for them. Consequently, she saw other females as a threat.

Thankfully, after well over forty years together, we are still best friends, lovers, care deeply for each other, and have learned to trust one another. Sure, we've each had opportunities to stray, but we haven't done it. We are also such good friends that we can *respectfully* joke about the other being hit on—especially when it's right in front of us.

To be truthful, as we get older this happens much less, if at all. Nonetheless, when it did, we'd congratulate each other with a wink and a smile for still 'having it.' Instead of being upset that your guy or gal is being hit on or checked out, be flattered that he or she chose you.

It's going to take a great deal of discipline to control jealousy, but respecting your partner starts with trust. Trust in the notion that he or she is likely flattered with the attention, but not interested. Congratulate him or her with a warm smile, just like a best friend would.

Our advice is to analyze the source of your jealousy. Are you acting self-centered? Are you looking at your partner as a piece of property instead of as a friend? If so, this isn't healthy and certainly isn't fair to your partner. Recognize that your partner is a friend and an independent person. Trust him or her unless he or she has given you reason not to.

Has your partner demonstrated behavior that genuinely justifies your emotion? If so, it's time to have a serious discussion with him or her. Honestly and respectfully lay out your concerns and feelings. Try to keep emotions in check during this discussion. Keep asking yourself, "Is this jealousy justified? Is there past evidence of betrayal, or is there good evidence for a suspicion of recent betrayal?" If so, then weigh the options and decide if this person is truly your friend. Was it one moment of stupidity, or is it the behavior of a narcissist? Agree on next steps and agree to follow up with further discussion and plans of action.

It has been our observation that straying often begins when couples stop communicating, fall out of friendship, or stop showing love to one another. Be sure you are following the 15 Rules to help you avoid a situation where your partner feels the need to stray. Moreover, be careful not to damage your relationship with unwarranted jealousy or accusations. Look in the mirror: do you think this way because of your partner's behavior, or is it insecurity on your part? Lead by example and follow the Rules. Be confident in the knowledge that your partner chose you.

Nobody can guarantee that your partner will follow along and be loyal. But if you are truly following *all* 15 Rules, then the onus is on them. It's their loss, not yours, and it's their fault, not yours. That's all you can do.

CHAPTER 15
Rule #14
Be Trustworthy

"Everyone must choose one of two pains: The pain of discipline or the pain of regret."

~ Jim Rohn ~
American entrepreneur, author, and motivational speaker
1930 - 2009

L et's face it: temptation is a powerful emotion. We all want to feel wanted, needed, and even lusted after. If someone is showing us attention, it can be tough to resist, especially when hormones kick in. And then there's the imagination; fantasies can be entertaining, to say the least. How do you avoid temptation when opportunity reveals itself at the most vulnerable moments?

The first step is to try to avoid those vulnerable moments. "That's easy to say," you might be thinking. "But damn, much like those other animalistic emotions, that's going to take one hell of a fight." YES, IT IS.

Much like we discussed before, sometimes an emotion only hurts the one who harbors it. So, unless you are a terribly cold-hearted person, the power of the *pain of regret* should be a strong incentive for avoiding a short-lived good time. Regret is another emotion that only tears at the soul of one who holds it, but it is also one that is difficult to release from our inner psyche. Perhaps you have long-held regrets that continue to cause you pain.

You Can't Have Your Cake and Eat it Too

Giving in to temptation will quite likely ruin your relationship. No matter how strong you think you are, it only takes a few minutes of weakness to destroy trust in a relationship. Be mindful of your strengths and weaknesses and plan accordingly.

If you are tempted, you must choose. A successful relationship takes total commitment, nothing less. Straying happens when one partner or the other isn't all-in. Not being fully committed to each other and all of the 15 Rules will likely lead to irreconcilable differences. Ask yourself whether you are fully committed to each other. Are you in or out? You can't have it both ways.

A Trusted Friend

Are you trustworthy? Can you be trusted when it comes to social media, your cell phone, or even your wallet or purse? Is there anything there that your partner shouldn't see? We can't imagine this, but we've even heard stories of one partner blocking the other on Facebook. What does the 'blocker' have to hide? What does it say about a relationship's strength when this occurs?

We've already established that the foundation for a successful relationship undoubtedly includes open communication, honesty, and trust. When you or your partner head down a different road, you are heading for trouble.

Our friend Maria and her husband know and share each other's Facebook and cell phone passwords.

"Without trust, there is nothing," she explained.

"There's no need to look at his cell phone, but it's comforting to know that I could if I wanted to," she continued. "Having both passwords was also a blessing when he was injured and in the hospital.

"That's love, trust, and friendship at its very core," she concluded.

Healthy relationships are about trust. Be trustworthy; be open; be respectful. Maria's husband can look in her purse if he wants to, but he wouldn't do it without asking first. The same rules apply for his wallet and his and her cell phones. There's no need to snoop because there's nothing to hide when you are trusting friends from the start.

Separate but Equal

The same standards apply for financial accounts. Before we were married, the advice from divorced friends and relatives was to have separate checking accounts because 'it gets ugly when you split up.'

We soundly rejected this advice, thinking that's no way to start a trusting relationship. Our only rule is big purchases (over $75) require communication beforehand. It's worked out so far, and most times we don't bounce a check.

Oscar and Marge, married almost sixty years, have a different spin. They have three checking accounts: one mutual account is for all the bills, plus they each have a separate account. Each gets a weekly allowance transferred into their personal checking account, which can be used any way they like.

Either way you choose, healthy relationships involve trust. Always be that trustworthy friend to your partner.

CHAPTER 16

Rule #15
Respect Life, Liberty, and The Pursuit of Happiness

"As you walk down the fairway of life you must smell the roses, for you only get to play one round."

~ Ben Hogan ~
American Professional Golfer
1927 - 1997

Steve and I are sure you've heard the relationship term, 'a keeper,' 'quite the catch,' and 'trophy wife.' All these phrases are widely viewed as and are meant to be compliments, but in a sense, they are also condescending. Psychologically speaking, it conjures up a vision that one's partner is a possession.

In Rules 1-14, we professed that your friend, lover, etc. is a partner in your life, that your happiness depends on their happiness, and that there *is* a great pleasure to be had from giving. Unequivocally your partner is not your property—he or she never has been and never will be. Although I joke that I have a marriage certificate saying that I own Steve, that is not the case; it's merely a rental agreement.

If You're Gonna Leave, Leave Now While I'm Still Young and Beautiful

One thing we've always said about each other is that we are so in love, and love one another so much, that we would never wish the other to spend a lifetime unhappy. As hard and heartbreaking as it would be, we've both told each other that it's okay to end the relationship if the other is unhappy or unsatisfied. We aren't each other's possession. We are each other's best friend and lover.

We each get only one crack at life. Life is short, fragile, and final. Don't get in the way of your partner's happiness; instead, make it a point to be the reason for it.

Dignity and respect operate along the same lines. Your partner always deserves your best. Leave no room to *ever* discount your partner's opinion, and have no tolerance for a cavalier attitude or condescending remarks. Your relationship is a partnership, so you are required to respect an opposing view, make all significant decisions together, and eschew negative comments while allowing for constructive communication

Be your partner's most enthusiastic cheerleader, even when they have come up with another crazy idea or proposal... again! Trust us; we've each had a few ourselves.

Be supportive. Together, we wrote this book. It was a crazy idea, but we did it. Your partner's crazy idea is or may very well turn into their passion. Are you going to discount your best friend's passion and destroy his or her dream?

We've won some and lost some in each of our searches for happiness, but we've never discounted each other's dreams...even Steve's silly ideas.

One, and Done

God has given us one precious life to live. Your partner has chosen to share that one very precious gift with you. Be grateful for your partner's generosity. In turn, know that he or she deserves and is entitled to experience a fulfilling life of their choice, with the understanding that they *"are created equal; ... endowed by their Creator with certain unalienable rights; that among these are life, liberty, and the pursuit of happiness..."*

These astoundingly beautiful and boldly written words, fashioned 250 years ago in the United States Declaration of Independence, still serve as a relevant reminder today of the precious gift of life given to all humans by their Creator. Whether we are referring to a nation or a relationship, we profess that this is a powerful creed.

CHAPTER 17
Final Thoughts

"You know you're in love when you can't fall asleep because reality is finally better than your dreams."

~ Dr. Seuss ~

American author, political cartoonist, illustrator, poet, animator, screenwriter, and filmmaker

1904 - 1991

"Rules, rules, rules, ugh! It's so stressful. How can we have any fun with all these rules?" You might be thinking. Geez, lighten up. We want you to have lots of fun and be successful in love and life. If you follow the Rules properly, you *will* have fun together.

Every day, we work hard on our relationship and keeping our 'flame' lit. Doing so is a daily task, but a task performed with enthusiasm, a smile, and rose-colored glasses. You've gotta keep it fun for both of you. We admit that not all of our Rules are a barrel of fun; however, many are, and they will put a spark in your relationship.

If you aren't doing it already, work on being each other's best friend. This may take getting out of your comfort zone, but it's the foundation to build the rest of the relationship. It's imperative.

What will you do today to start your new friendship or to improve your existing friendship? What can you do to make your friend smile today? Be committed to giving happiness and love. Happiness and love beget happiness and love. Try it! It's contagious, and you won't regret it.

Give all of yourself and commit 100% to your relationship. Lead by example, using every one of these 15 Rules we've laid out. Hold up your end of the bargain. Our professional experience has demonstrated that leading by example is most often the best way to get positive results.

And, good heavens, stop sweating the small stuff. Moreover, stop doing those little things that drive your partner crazy—at least the ones that you *can* change. Life is too short to stress over this small stuff. Focus on the positives in your relationship. Smile at the mistakes and minor irritants. A word of caution, however...be sure to turn your head away to smile if that smile is going to piss him or her off.

Remember to compliment often. Say something nice, and be creative about it. If you have that overwhelming urge to critique, say, for 'educational purposes,' use the sandwich approach:

Compliment
Constructive criticism
Compliment

Happiness is derived from inside you, and from giving. Give praise, give compliments, give love.

Winning an argument is not like winning a battle. Every argument needs a peacemaker. Lead by example; tone it down until it becomes a negotiation, not a war, with perhaps a compromise that results in mutual agreement and satisfaction. Stay calm to avoid those words or actions that hurt. Winning the battle but losing the war is always a possibility. Choose words carefully, breathe, count to ten—a moment of extended silence is far better than a quick response you are bound to regret later. Bite your lip until it bleeds to avoid doing permanent damage to your relationship.

Unfortunately, despite your very best efforts, you will be wrong sometimes. Have the courage to show love and respect to your partner by fessing up to your wrongdoings, mistakes, and misstatements. It's not that bad; really, it's refreshing and usually good for extra 'brownie points' with your partner.

Avoid blaming. Here too, there is the risk of saying something you can't take back. Plus, the negative feelings you keep locked inside of you only hurt and harm you. Relieve yourself of this burden. When you truly forgive, you literally feel a weight lifted off your shoulders. We've done it, and it's heavenly.

Fun, fun, fun! Have fun with your best friend. Have fun with an experience that goes as expected, and have even more fun when things go wrong. Laugh with and love your best friend everywhere and every day. Don't take yourself so damn seriously, 'cuz you ain't that important, and being serious ain't no fun.

Accept your best friend, your partner, your lover, for who they are, not who want them to be. They should be comfortable being themselves. You, too, should be comfortable being yourself—a first-rate version of yourself, of course—not one that's grumpy or self-centered. If that's you, then knock it off and *carefully* re-read the 15 Rules.

Look to find shared interests and go out on a limb to discover new adventures. You may be surprised.

Be thankful your partner chose you, and don't let jealousy ruin each other's day, week, month or relationship. Lighten up and take pleasure if your partner receives a little attention. Compliment him or her and point out the attention inconspicuously with a whisper or an elbow when it's only you who notices. Smile and laugh about it later. After all, this 'catch' chose to be with you. And for heaven's sake, watch to avoid those tempting moments that can screw it all up for good.

Be sure to respect your partner's personhood. It's a partnership, not a one-sided affair. *Happy wife, happy life,* so they say, but let's not forget the guys too, 'cuz it's gotta be equal.

That's it in a nutshell. It ain't rocket surgery or anything like that. But seriously, it takes real dedication to create a loving, lasting, and satisfying relationship.

In the end, our Rules encompass simple human dignity and respect. Merely treating your partner and other fellow humans with dignity, respect, kindness, love, compassion, and friendliness will help you be successful.

If you are already practicing all these 15 Rules, congratulations on what is likely a beautiful relationship, and congratulations for achieving what seems to be lacking lately. If you are still seeking this type of relationship, we dearly hope you find it.

In closing, we'd like to leave you with these words. As our hair has turned from vibrant to gray, we have gained knowledge that only experience can bring. We've learned life's lessons, both good and bad. Over the years, and much too rapidly for our liking, our appearance has gone from youthful to weathered, and it would seem our souls have experienced the same. However, although they are weathered, they are not hardened.

We have learned that the real treasures in life are the things you can't hold in your hands. Having material 'stuff' is nice, but the most valuable assets you have are the memories and love you've shared with friends and family.

We have loved and lost more family members and friends than we wish to count. Some were taken in the winter of their lives; their sunsets were inevitable and not surprising. We can be somewhat comforted in the knowledge that their demise is the natural order of things. This understanding lessens the shock a bit, but it certainly doesn't mitigate the loss. Some loved ones were taken much too young. These deaths were more devastating, because in addition to the great sense of loss and shock, they heightened our awareness of life's fragility. As these losses piled up, we realized that the most cherished 'possessions' are friendship and love. If you lose these treasures, all you are left with is memories and emptiness.

In our roles working in skilled nursing facilities, we had the pleasure of meeting hundreds of elders, many of whom were restricted to a wheelchair and relied solely on nurses and other caregivers for all their basic human needs. All had but a few worldly possessions left to their names, but the 'value' of these goods seemingly diminishes when one's health and independence withers away.

Therefore, those elders who invested in their relationships appear to be 'richer' and more tranquil. For those who were fortunate to have a partner who visited or shared a room, their togetherness was an absolute treasure. It was a beautiful sight, to see how a warm smile, hug, or an eagerly performed chore united two into one.

If you take the time, each of these nursing home residents is eager to tell of days gone by and the fond memories they shared with their partner, even when that significant other has passed. Very few focus solely on their accomplishments or obtained assets, but all who had a satisfying relationship reminisce about it.

With this knowledge, it is quite evident that it may well be worth the effort to strive for a loving, lasting, and satisfying relationship. We wish you well.

If you have any questions or comments, we'd love to hear from you. Good luck and God Bless.

Janet and Steve

ABOUT THE AUTHORS

A Registered Nurse and healthcare executive, Janet Hall is highly respected in her industry and responsible for the development of many healthcare-related policies.

A healthcare executive, inventor, voice actor, and award-winning speaker, Steven Hall has been credited with helping to develop a groundbreaking healthcare management program and two healthcare safety devices.

Janet and Steve, who reside in Central Massachusetts, will tell you that their biggest joy comes from spending time with their family, including their five grandchildren. Ma and Papa, as they are known, are often seen at the grandkids' sporting events, or skiing or dirt biking with them.

REFERENCES

Jegede, A. (2019, January 21). *Top 10 Countries With Highest Divorce Rates.* Retrieved from TRENDRR: https://www.trendrr.net/8004/countries-with-highest-divorce-rate-world-famous-lowest-india-japan/#10_United_States_of_America-divorce_rate_53

Wikipedia.org (2019, november 23). *Gilligan's Island.* Retrieved from Wikipedia: https://en.wikipedia.org/wiki/Gilligan%27s_Island#Ginger_or_Mary_Ann.3F

Audubon, Massachusetts (2019). *snake-species-in-massachusetts.* Retrieved from Mass Audubon: https://www.massaudubon.org/learn/nature-wildlife/reptiles-amphibians/snakes/snake-species-in-massachusetts

Mount Washington Observatory (2019). *World Record Wind.* Retrieved 25 October 2019 at https://www.mountwashington.org/about-us/history/world-record-wind.aspx

Made in the USA
Middletown, DE
21 December 2019